Learn Guitar Fast!

Looking After Your Guitar

Everyday Maintenance and Repairs

Richard Riley, Harry Wylie

Produced and created by
FLAME TREE PUBLISHING
Crabtree Hall, Crabtree Lane
Fulham, London, SW6 6TY
United Kingdom
www.flametreepublishing.com

First Published 2004

Publisher and Creative Director: Nick Wells
Editorial: Julia Rolf, Polly Willis
Designer: Jake

Special thanks to Matt McArdle for the additional
photographs

07 06 05 04
10 9 8 7 6 5 4 3 2 1

ISBN 1 84451 132 4

© 2004 Flame Tree Publishing
Flame Tree Publishing is part of the Foundry Creative Media
Company Limited

Introduction

Be it a Gibson Les Paul or a flamenco model, a guitar is for life, not just for Christmas. To get the best results out of your guitar you will need to treat it with the care and attention it deserves. Guitars sometimes end up getting a bit of a rough ride – just consider the tragic fates of most of Pete Townshend's early instruments – but even if you are constantly gigging and swapping around instruments, it is important to keep up a certain level of guitar maintenance.

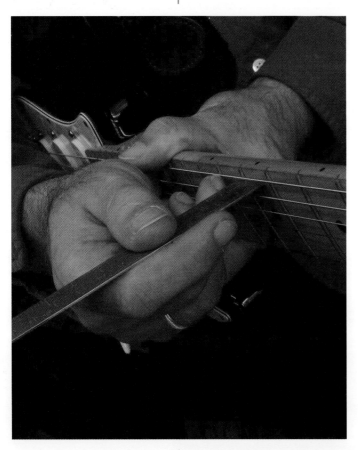

This book is divided into two sections; the first examines the guitar itself, how the instrument is constructed and its various constituent parts, from the headstock down to the tailpiece. You cannot be a surgeon without knowledge of the human anatomy and, in the same way, it is a great help to know how your guitar fits together before you attempt to take it apart for repairs. You can also discover how variations in the way a guitar is made can alter the sound it produces, as well as the instrument's outward appearance.

The second section concentrates on how to repair and look after your guitar. It is useful to be able to carry out your own repairs – think of all the money and trips to the repair shop you will save yourself! This book guides you through a variety of guitar maintenance and repair procedures with the aid of illustrations, from the simple tasks of fretboard care, protecting your guitar from bumps and cleaning your instrument to more complex and technical repairs such as replacing a pickup or jack socket. Both acoustic and electric guitars are covered, so whether you are a folkie or a metaller, this book can offer invaluable guidance on keeping your guitar in good condition.

Contents

The Guitar

Care and Maintenance

The Guitar

Construction Materials

The choice of woods used in guitar construction is essential to the final sound. Some makers have tried alternatives: Perspex, graphite, even aluminium. But nothing beats wood for sustain, resonance and natural strength.

The Fender Telecaster is two pieces of ash bolted together, while Gibson's Les Paul uses a mahogany body with maple top. For acoustic guitars, the harder the wood for the back and sides, the brighter the sound. Thin solid woods are best for acoustic resonance and strength. Traditionally, the back and sides of a guitar are made of a hardwood, such as rosewood. Alternatives include koa, mahogany, maple or bovinga. The neck uses a strong wood resistant to bending, such as mahogany or maple. The face or soundboard is always made of a softwood, such as sitka or another kind of spruce, which flexes to produce sound waves which the harder back and sides echo and amplify. Nowadays, plywoods and laminates are used on cheaper instruments as wood supplies become more expensive. Some makers are also championing the use of 'smart woods' as world supplies of choice hardwoods become scarcer.

Maple

Commonly used in the fingerboards and necks of Fender solid-bodies, such as the Telecaster or Stratocaster. It is also an alternative to rosewood for the finest quality resonance.

BELOW: As well as being beautiful wood, maple is easy to work with and has good elasticity, which has made it popular for musical instrument construction.

Mahogany

The inventor of the first Gibson solid-body, Les Paul, used mahogany to achieve a natural sustain of 25 seconds. These guitars are still known for their legendary sustain.

ABOVE: Soundboards are made of spruce, which combines strength with lightness.

Spruce

The wood most commonly found as the soundboard of good-quality acoustic instruments. Reasonably soft, it gives natural projection to the final sound. Pine is a similar replacement.

Korina

This is the trademark name for African limba wood, used on many Gibson models from the late 1950s onwards.

Rosewood

A heavy, expensive wood, rosewood is commonly used in the manufacture of guitar fingerboards.

ABOVE: Prized for its sustain, mahogany has been used in guitar construction since the 1900s.

Other Construction Materials

- **Brass.** Traditionally, the bridge or nut was made from of bone, ivory or mother-of-pearl. Most production models use plastic equivalents. Some electric players choose to upgrade the plastic nut to a brass model. This gives better sustain, a brighter tone, and can increase tuning reliability.

- **Bone.** Some players choose to upgrade the plastic nut of a modern acoustic guitar to ivory or bone. This gives better sustain and can increase tuning reliability.

- **Graphite.** Many players have found the hard-wearing qualities of graphite give the nut a much better sustain and tuning reliability than plastic alternatives. Other alternatives to bridge and nut materials include micarta and corion.

ABOVE: There is one tuning peg per string on the headstock. A knob extends from each peg, which is rotated to change the pitch of the string.

Headstock

The headstock is the structure at the end of a guitar's neck onto which the machine heads or tuning pegs are mounted. It is usually the part of the guitar that carries the manufacturer's name and logo, plus any other significant details of the guitar model. Headstocks vary greatly in design: some, such as those on the Fender Stratocaster and Telecaster guitars, have all of the machine heads mounted on one side while others, including the Gibson Les Paul and ES-335 models, have three on one side and three on the other.

Tuning Head

Each string of the guitar is attached to a tuning head (also known as a machine head). The tuning head has a string post through which the string is passed, and a button, used to turn the post either left or right. The button is connected to the post by a high ratio gear. This apparatus enables the player to fine tune the guitar. Budget tuning heads may have a simple mechanism while more expensive tuning heads have sealed gear chambers and very fine movement.

ABOVE: The tuning head, or machine head, can vary from the very simple to the highly complex, and is used to tune the strings.

Truss Rod

The truss rod is a metal bar used for reinforcing and adjusting a steel-strung guitar's neck. It can be adjusted to keep the neck straight if the tension changes when different gauge strings are used. One end of the truss rod is secured firmly to the heel (body end) of the neck and the other end is usually found beneath a cover-plate in the headstock, where it can be adjusted. Some guitars, notably Martin acoustics, have fixed truss rods that cannot be adjusted by the user.

BELOW: The truss rod of a Fender Stratocaster (seen centre of picture), which is used to reinforce its neck and keep it straight.

Capstan

Also known as a string post, the capstan is a round structure in a tuning head, usually made of steel, around which a string is wound. The whole structure is housed on the headstock of the guitar. When putting a new string on a guitar, make sure it is wrapped tightly and neatly several times around the capstan to ensure the guitar stays reliably in tune, especially if the type of playing to be done includes bending a lot of notes.

Nut

The nut is a structure at the headstock end of the fingerboard that the strings pass over before they reach the machine heads or pegs. The strings rest on the nut, and all string vibrations occur between here and the guitar's bridge. The nut also sets the strings' height above the fingerboard. It is traditionally made out of bone or ivory but most cheap guitar models have plastic ones fitted. Some guitars have a 'zero fret' fitted just in front of the nut. In such cases, the fret sets the string height at the headstock end of the guitar.

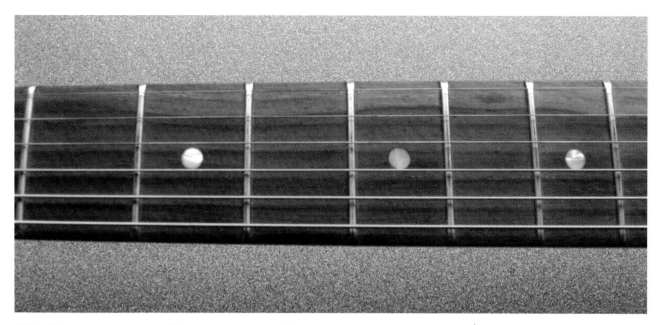

Fingerboard

The fingerboard, or fretboard, is attached to the front of the guitar neck and extends from the nut to the very end of the neck. Frets are fitted at very precise points on the fingerboard to enable the guitar player to accurately stop the string. The fingerboard is almost always made from wood. Maple, rosewood and ebony are often used in the manufacture of the fingerboard. As hardwood stocks are depleted manufacturers are finding new materials for the fingerboard. Many guitar players believe that the material used for the fingerboard has an effect on the tone of the guitar.

ABOVE: The fingerboard has 22 or so frets; the first fret is the first one down from the nut, unless there is one immediately after the nut, which is called the zero fret.

Fret

Frets are metal strips placed across the radius of a guitar's fingerboard to mark out notes a semitone apart. They make it easy for a guitarist to find precise notes in scales and chords. Frets come in all shapes and sizes: some are narrow while others are wide; and some are flat at the top while others are rounded. Some bass players prefer fretless basses for their more fluid sound. Fretless six-string guitars, however, are rarely used in popular music.

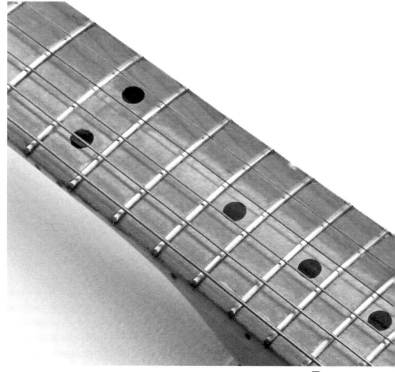

Crown

The crown is the top of a fret on the guitar fingerboard. Crowns vary in width and curvature, and these differences influence the tone of a vibrating string: a thin crown tends to give a crisp, treble edge to a string's tone, while a thicker one produces a more mellow sound that would appeal to a jazz player. Some crowns are rounded while others are flat, and these features also influence the tone of a guitar. A manufacturer will often stick to using a particular type of crown for their guitars: Fender electrics tend to have thin, rounded crowns while Gibsons usually have flat, wider ones.

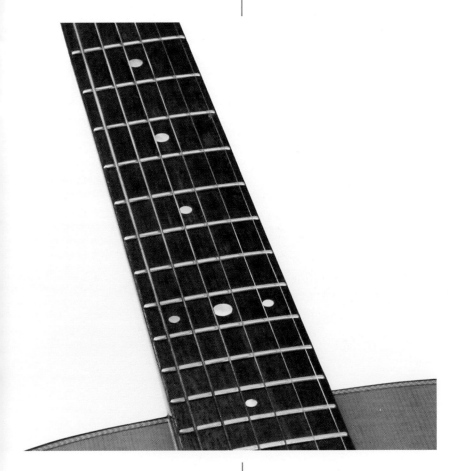

Dot Marker

Most guitars have markers along the neck to help players navigate the fingerboard. The most common markers are dots behind the 3rd, 5th, 7th, 9th, 15th, 17th, 19th and 21st frets, along with two dots behind the 12th fret to highlight the notes one octave higher than those on the open strings. Other common markers are blocks (commonly found on Gibson and Ibanez guitars) and 'shark-tooths' (used on rock guitar models such as the Jackson Soloist). Markers are usually made out of abalone or plastic.

Radius

The radius of a guitar fingerboard can be described as the curvature of the neck from the high E string to the low E string. If you took a ruler and put a point at one edge and a pencil at the other end and drew a circle, then cut out the width of the fretboard along the circumference of the circle, you would get the radius. Some guitars have completely flat fingerboards, and therefore no radius.

Cut Away

This is a rounded area cut out of a guitar's body next to the neck so that a player can comfortably reach further up the neck. Guitars such as Gibson Les Pauls and Fender Telecasters have cut aways underneath the neck, while others, including the Gibson SG, Gibson 335, Fender Stratocaster and numerous Paul Reed Smith models, have cut aways above and below the neck. The advantage of the latter is obvious: with a double cut away you can easily reach high notes on the top and bottom strings of the fingerboard, giving a much larger range of notes to the virtuoso player. Popular acoustics made by Ovation and Takamine also have cut aways.

Strings

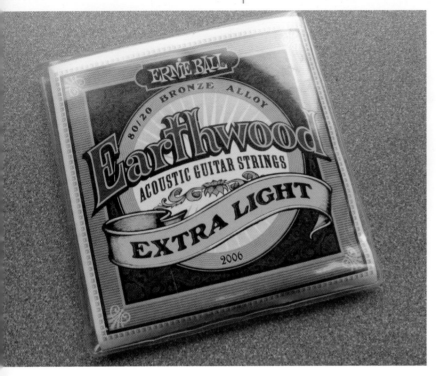

Bronze Strings

Guitar strings were traditionally made from either wire or gut, but nowadays there are just two main types: steel and nylon. Bronze, or phosphor bronze, strings are of the steel variety and are usually used with acoustic guitars. The sixth through to the fourth string will typically be wound – a solid steel core with bronze wound around the outside – while the first and second strings, the lowest gauges, will be plain steel. There are various manners of winding available, all of which give the instrument a different feel and tone. Round-wound strings are the most common.

Flat-Wound And Ground-Wound Strings

The answer to the problem of the unwanted fret noise caused by the grooved, uneven surface of round-wound strings is the flat-wound string, which uses flat steel tape or ribbon instead of wire, and thus eliminates the grooves. This produces a mellow tone and feel, perfect for jazz musicians. Ground-wound strings use the same construction methods as ordinary round-wounds, but are flattened or ground down to produce a smooth surface.

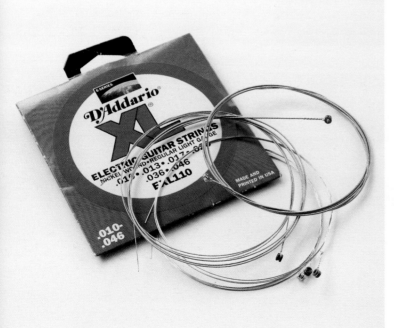

String Gauge

The gauge of a string is the technical term for its width or thickness, measured in thousandths of an inch. Typically, a set of six guitar strings will be referred to by the thickness of the first or highest string. Therefore a set of '10' gauge strings, considered to be the standard width for most electric players, will consist of a thinnest string of 0.010 in and five further strings of varying gauges to give a corresponding tension across the neck.

Gold Strings

Most strings used on a guitar consist of a solid steel core and a winding of either silver or bronze alloys. Silver strings usually use stainless steel for their winding, as this resonates within the magnetic field of the pickup of an electric guitar, producing an electric tone. Gold or bronze wound strings are more typically found on acoustic guitars. Bronze wound strings do not allow as much magnetic resonance and thus require a different amplification method, usually based on piezo crystals.

Nylon Strings

Nylon strings are used on classical guitars. They produce a much softer tone than steel or bronze strings and create less tension on the guitar's neck. The first stringed instruments used strings made of stretched cat gut, although traditionally a sheep's or pig's intestine would have been used. Nowadays, you can buy nylon equivalents which come in hard, medium or light gauges, and in ball end or loop varieties.

Round-Wound Strings

Over the nylon core of classical strings or the nickel core of steel strings, a wound loop of steel can be placed to increase the diameter of the string. The greater the diameter, the lower the note produced when the string is plucked under tension. The most common form is the round-wound variety. It is produced literally by spinning the core of the string as wire is fed out to cover it. The slight grooves between the windings of each thread of wire give the string an uneven surface, and can cause unwanted fret noise when sliding between notes.

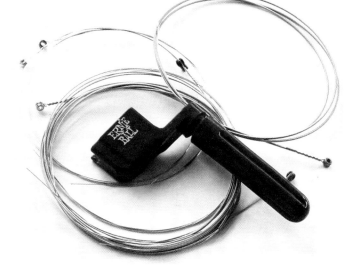

ABOVE: Different kinds of guitars use different strings, and each type produces a different sound. Pictured are steel strings, which are used on electric guitars.

Steel Strings

Steel or nickel strings are used on electric guitars. The thicker gauges, normally reserved for the first, second and third strings, will consist of a solid steel core wound with nickel, steel or even gold. The highest three strings will be solid steel or nickel. The strings come in various thicknesses, or gauges, designed to be tuned up to the six notes of standard tuning, EADGBE. Each string can be tuned up to a whole tone higher than its intended note, but any more stretching may result in string breakage or neck damage.

Soundhole

The soundhole is the hole in the front of the guitar body through which sound projects from the soundchamber. Most acoustic guitar soundholes are round, although some are oval (as on early Gibson acoustics), D-shaped (as on Maccaferri guitars), or violin-like f-holes (as on the Gibson ES-350). Semi-acoustic guitars, such as the Gibson ES-335 and ES-355 models, also have f-holes. Acoustic guitar soundholes are usually surrounded by attractively decorated inlays made out of different woods, bone, plastic or abalone.

F-Hole

F-holes are soundholes found on a number of acoustic and electric guitars. Early Gibson acoustic models, archtops such as the L-5 (first produced during the 1920s) and Super 400 (made during the 1930s), were among the first guitars to feature f-holes. A more recent model, the Gibson-335, introduced in 1957 and played by everyone from Chuck Berry to Noel Gallagher, is a semi-acoustic guitar with f-holes. Some guitars, such as the Gretsch Chet Atkins 1962 reissue model, have simulated f-holes painted onto the body as an ornamental decoration.

Scratchplate

A scratchplate is a plastic plate fixed to the lower-front part of a guitar's body (underneath the soundhole on an acoustic steel-string instrument) to protect it from wear and tear caused by the player's plectra or finger-picks. They can also serve an ornamental purpose and are sometimes adorned with intricate inlays, engravings and decoration. Some players do not have scratchplates on their guitars because they feel, with some justification, that they compromise the tone of the soundboard. Classical and flamenco guitars do not have scratchplates.

Soundboard

The soundboard or top supports the bridge. The soundboard is made of carved or planed wood, finely tuned and shaped to vibrate when the strings are plucked. Vibrations from the strings are carried by the top to the body of the guitar where they are amplified by the shape of the guitar. The thin soundboard is made to vibrate by the movement of air inside the body and in turn enables tiny vibrations of the string to be heard.

Bridge

This part of the guitar, along with the saddle, transmits energy from the string vibrations to the body of the guitar. It also spreads the mechanical tension of the strings. There are two main types of bridge: a fixed bridge, which is glued to the top of the soundboard with the strings anchored to it; and a floating bridge, which is held in place only by the tension in the strings that pass over it. Both types of bridge are usually made of metal, or high-density woods such as ebony or rosewood that aid sustain and vibration transfer to the body. Floating bridges can be moved to adjust the intonation if necessary.

Binding

Binding, or edge binding, is a protective strip fitted along the outside edges of the guitar soundbox where it joins with the sides of the guitar body. The binding keeps the pieces of wood that make up the guitar's body firmly joined together and reduces vibrations from occurring within the soundboard and back panel. It can also serve as a decorative effect and the binding on some guitars includes inlaid ornate materials, such as mother-of-pearl or ivory.

Saddle

The saddle is the place on a guitar's bridge for supporting the strings. The distance between it and the nut determines the scale length (length of vibrating open string) of a guitar. Acoustic guitars tend to have a one-piece saddle, made of bone or plastic, fixed at a slightly slanting angle so that the intonation of all six strings is correct. Electric-guitar saddles usually have six substructures, each with a groove over which a string passes. Some guitars have adjustable saddles that can be lowered or raised to alter their action.

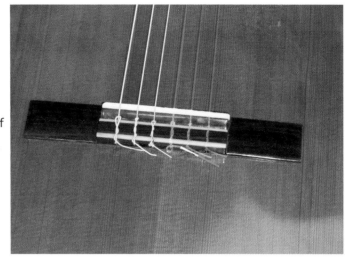

ABOVE: Saddle of a Spanish guitar.

ABOVE: Saddle of an electric guitar.

Tailpiece

Some guitars have a tailpiece, which is a wooden or metal frame for holding the strings at the body end of the guitar. On such guitars the strings are fixed at the tailpiece and usually pass over a floating bridge attached to the guitar's body. The tailpiece was a prominent feature on archtop guitars, which first appeared during the 1920s and were hugely popular through to the late 1950s. Most modern guitars have their strings attached at a fixed bridge to pass over a saddle on or close to the bridge on the guitar's body.

BELOW: The decorative tailpiece of a Rickenbacker 360.

Care & Maintenance

Cleaning Your Guitar

Keeping your guitar in good order is very important, and cleaning it every time you play is an essential part of this process.

Firstly, always use a soft cloth to wipe down the strings after playing, and try pulling the strings away from the fingerboard and letting go a couple of times to dislodge any dirt build-up. This will dramatically extend their lifespan, and make the guitar much more playable the next time you pick it up.

Secondly, use a non-abrasive cloth to wipe down the neck and body of the guitar, especially metal areas such as pickup covers and machine-heads, which can easily rust or tarnish if left damp or unprotected. You can use any household spray polish on the lacquered body of your electric or acoustic guitar to remove grubby finger-marks and smears, and you can also use a similar cream or spray on the fingerboard. Make sure you clean the polish off thoroughly and work it well into the grain.

Guitars with French-polish or oiled finishes (particularly classical guitars) will need to be cleaned with special oils and polish. If your guitar is of this type, ask your dealer what materials you should and should not use on it.

String Cleaner

The more a guitar is played, the more dirt and grease will be deposited on the strings. There are three accepted ways of cleaning strings. The first is to use a soft cloth before and after you play and to keep your hands as clean as possible. The second is to raise the strings and 'snap' them back into position regularly, to help dislodge dirt build-up. You can also try removing strings and boiling them in water, although few players nowadays bother with this method. The last technique is to use a proprietary string cleaner, such as Fast-Fret, which employs a special liquid compound to reduce the build-up of grime and keep the string smooth.

LEFT: Cleaning your guitar is a very good habit to get into.

Storing Your Guitar

Acoustic and electric guitars are comfortable being stored in a dry room with low humidity and even temperature. Avoid hanging your guitar on the wall, especially over a radiator as this will dry the guitar out. In the winter store your guitar inside with a humidifier inside the case. Keep the guitar away from direct sunlight to avoid spoiling the finish. Invest in a quality guitar-stand and keep your guitar on its stand anywhere that you feel comfortable.

ABOVE: A glass of water left in a centrally heated room can stop guitars drying out.

Travelling With Your Guitar

Many options are available for protecting your guitar against damage while travelling. For most purposes a heavily padded bag will provide protection against normal knocks and travelling wear and have the advantage of shoulder straps and additional pockets. If your guitar will be out of sight it is vital to invest in either a moulded plastic case or a heavy duty wooden and metal flight case. The case should always be locked and an inventory of the contents, with a picture and a record of all serial numbers should be kept with you. Place packets of moisture absorbent gel in the case.

Case

Every guitar needs at some time or other to be stored safely, away from damp, dirt and general destruction. There are a number of options for safely storing your guitar, and most dealers will supply one or the other with the instrument when it is sold. The most basic is a simple vinyl covering with a zip around the outer edge. This affords the guitar no structural protection whatsoever, but will at least make it easier to transport and keep it free of dust. Far more reliable is the gig bag, which is a hefty, padded nylon or cloth casing. A gig bag will usually also include straps so the guitar can be carried on your back, and outside pockets so you can store useful gadgets or spare strings. Lastly, a hard case is the heaviest but safest option for transporting your instrument safely. Some, such as the Gibson variety, come moulded to the shape of the instrument and include a silk cover for protecting its surface; others come in simple rectangular shapes, often lushly finished in foam and soft nylon padding.

Woodwork And General Repairs

Specialist equipment is available for guitar repair although a basic toolkit can be assembled from stock at your local DIY superstore. If you do not have a workbench then make a portable MDF workplace that can be clamped to a table and to which vices and other fixings can be attached.

Keep a small number of craft knives for trimming and shaping and a good stock of very sharp Stanley knife blades. These are essential for scraping, shaving and cutting.

White PVA wood glue can be used for repairs to soundboards and replacing nuts although structural neck and bridge repair requires specialist glues from guitar parts suppliers.

A selection of hand clamps should be available as well as a large number of very strong elastic bands, useful when repairing binding. A modeller's saw and modellers files are essential for fine finishing and repairing and a small Swiss hammer can be useful when fitting parts.

Always keep a stock of quality medium and fine grit sandpapers and a number of fine grade synthetic steel wool pads for rubbing down. Purchase a hand-smoothing plane and learn how to make a sharp edge using an oil stone to keep chisels and other cutting tools in top condition.

BELOW: Keep a good supply of tools on hand so it is easy to make that vital repair to your guitar.

Spare Parts

Keep a selection of commonly broken or lost parts such as top nuts (both electric and acoustic), machine heads (never throw old ones out) , screws and strap buttons, bridge pins, etc. For electric instruments keep replacement switches and switch caps, a good stock of spare pots (potentiometers) both 250 and 500 Ohm plus capacitors for tone controls. Jack sockets frequently fail but are very quick to replace so long as you have a few in stock complete with mounting plates for Gibson-style guitars.

Electrical problems can be quickly traced with a simple resistance meter and always keep a complete set of Allen (hex) keys in both imperial (for US guitars) and metric (for everyone else's). An electric guitar tuner is invaluable for setting up and resolving intonation problems, and is even more useful if you use a tuner with a needle display rather than segment LEDS for precision.

ABOVE: Having spare parts for your guitar saves you wasting valuable playing time visiting the repair shop to buy them.

Fast Winder

Many players find changing strings quite a pleasant and therapeutic business, and once you have the technique down to a fine art, it is not overly time-consuming to change routinely all six strings. For some players, however, time is essential in performing a string change – particularly for professional roadies or guitar technicians who might have to change the strings of many guitars every day, or who might have to change a vital broken string in between the songs of a live set. A fast winder is a simple device that lets you quickly wind the capstan of the tuning peg with a single, smooth, easy turning action. Many players also prefer this technique, as it helps wind the string more evenly than turning the machine head manually. Some roadies will even use converted power drills to wind on strings very quickly.

Repairing A Bridge

Loose or lifting bridges are common on older acoustic guitars. The bridge may become loose if glue degrades or if a crack has developed under the bridge. Sometimes incorrect use of very heavy gauge strings will damage the bridge and the guitar top. Before attempting this kind of repair it is very important to remove the strings from the guitar and leave it in its case for about a week. This will enable the guitar to relax back into shape.

Take the guitar and work a thin flexible blade under the bridge and gradually ease the bridge from the guitar, taking great care not to damage the top. Do not use any form of heat, steam injection or similar. Some damage and tearing is inevitable. Leave the wood attached to the bottom of the bridge as this will assist you when you come to replacing the bridge.

When the bridge is removed you can clean up the area around and under the bridge removing any old glue etc. Reglue the bridge using Titebond repairers glue or similar animal-based glue (white PVA glue is not strong enough) and clamp firmly in place while the glue dries.

Repairing A Solid-Top Guitar

Controls are mounted through the wood on Gibson-style guitars. Excessive force can knock controls through the guitar top and leave a ragged hole in the guitar.

Remove the control plates behind the hole and make a sketch of the parts and connections before removing the electronics (keeping as many connections intact as possible). Trim and clean the hole using a craft knife, leaving as much wood as possible. Clean around the hole inside the guitar and on the surface. Cover the hole inside the guitar with a piece of masking tape.

Make up a small amount of automotive body filler and work into the damage; the tape will stop it falling through into the control cavity. Allow to completely cure, then rub down using medium, then fine sandpaper before finishing with T-Cut.

Create a new hole for the control knob using a high speed drill and a suitable bit to make a hole just larger than the shaft of the control. Push the control through the body and reattach before replacing the control knob. A satisfactory partial spray refinishing of a solid body guitar is almost impossible to achieve, so aim to create a very small area for filling, and if possible fit larger control knobs to cover the filled area.

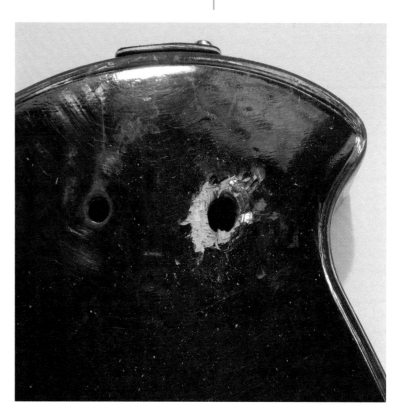

Guitar Finish

BELOW: Sunburst finish.

BELOW: Polyester finish.

The finish of your guitar is the high-gloss coat of coloured lacquer or plastic covering the body and the back of the neck. Depending on the age and make of your guitar the finish will either be a heavy coat of polyurethane, catalysed lacquer or polyester. The finish may either be a solid colour or a graduated finish called a Sunburst.

Finishes are usually high-gloss although satin and oil finishes are common. Manufacturers strive to achieve the best finish in the shortest possible time and adopt high technology such as curing with ultra-violet light.

Care for the finish of your guitar by buffing immediately after each practise with a soft cloth and a top-quality instrument preparation such as Jim Dunlops Formula 65. Minor scratches can be rubbed out with a little effort and some mild abrasive metal polish such as Brasso or automotive finishers.

Repairing Finish And Refinishing

Minor scratches and abrasions can be rubbed out using T-Cut and an old cotton shirt.

Take a piece of the shirt (without buttons) and rub vigorously around and over the scratch. Apply a small teaspoon of T-Cut to the scratch and gently rub in small circles using the cotton cleaning cloth. Apply light pressure to avoid generating heat. When you are satisfied that you cannot remove it any further repeat the process with Brasso to restore the high gloss. Finally buff with a soft cloth and Formula 65.

The guitar body can be completely refinished using automotive spray paint. Strip the guitar down and remove all hardware, pickups and covers leaving just the guitar body. Les Paul and other set neck guitars require the fingerboard to be heavily masked. The neck on Fender-style guitars can be completely removed. Sand the entire body using medium and fine grade sandpaper then suspend the body using wire or rope through the neck screw holes or machine head holes. Apply spray paint very thinly leaving at least six hours to dry between coats. The painted body must then be left for at least two days before final rubbing with T-Cut.

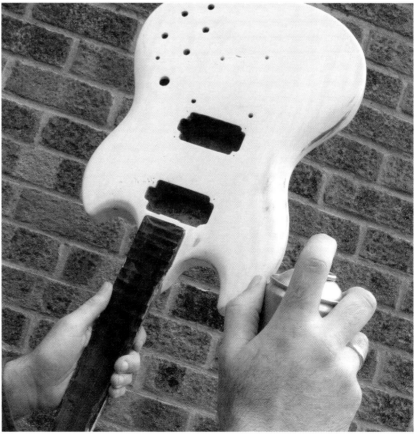

Fretboard Care

ABOVE: Your guitar's fretboard can accumulate a lot of dirt and grease from your fingers, so it is important to clean it regularly.

This procedure is not suitable for instruments with varnished fingerboards. Remove the strings and scrape rough dirt from the board with a clean cotton cloth until the wood is dry and clean. Take a piece of 000-gauge synthetic steel wool and gently rub over the length of the fingerboard. Take care not to press too hard – imagine you are brushing the coat of a dog. After a short time, the frets will become bright and the grain of the fingerboard will become clear.

Using your fingernail or a plectrum behind a thin piece of cotton or some kitchen wipes, remove residue trapped between the fret and fingerboard along the length of the neck. Wipe over the neck with a piece of clean cotton lightly dampened with prepared lemon oil or a very small amount of good-quality olive oil. Buff vigorously with a cotton cloth until frets and fingerboard are glossy.

Fret File

A fret file is a simple device for sanding down uneven or protruding frets on your guitar. It can also be used to smooth off the edges of badly finished or new frets at the edges of the guitar neck.

There is an easy way of discovering if any of the frets are too high on the neck of your guitar, but first you must check that there are no other problems, such as a badly set action (string height) or a warped neck (see pages 34 and 35 for how to do this).

To check your frets, play each fret on each string one at a time. A high fret will cause a buzzing sound when you play the fret below it. To file it down, use a fret file in a smooth easy action, working up and down the neck. Check frequently that you do not file too much off, or that you do not file down the surrounding frets too. A curved fret file can then be used to recreate the exact camber of the surrounding frets. Then restring the guitar and check again for buzzes along the neck. If in doubt about performing this kind of guitar surgery, take the instrument to your nearest dealer, who should be able to recommend a reliable guitar technician.

Fixing Loose Frets

A loose fret can cause string buzzing. Tap the loose fret back into place using a small Swiss hammer or remove carefully using pliers and replace with fresh wire. When replacing the fret, clean the slot and apply a very small amount of white glue before cutting a new fret, slotting it into place and tapping it down. Leave it to dry overnight, then finish off the top of the fret with a crowning file and finally smooth it with steel wool or synthetic pad. Don't forget to smooth the fret where it appears at the side of the fingerboard.

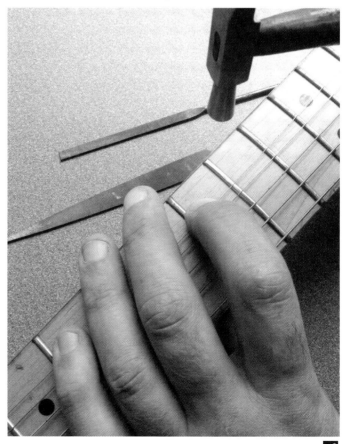

String Care

Why Do Strings Break?

Steel and nylon guitar strings break as the material used to make the string breaks down over time through a combination of fatigue, tension and corrosion. The most common place for steel strings to break is over the bridge saddle, as this is where the player's hand will rest. Acid in sweat reacts with the metal to cause corrosion and reduce the ability of the metal string to withstand the high tension needed to keep the string in tune. Sharp edges on the saddle can also cut the string. Periodically run a small piece of fine emery paper over each saddle to keep them smooth.

How To Make Strings Last Longer

Increase the life of your strings by applying a fine coat of 3-in-1 oil to each saddle before you fit the new string. The thin oil will be trapped under the string and prevent moisture from creeping between the string and the saddle. After you have fitted your new strings wipe a soft cloth dipped in a little 3-in-1 over the strings and saddles. As well as prolonging the life of your strings the oil will keep intonation and height adjustment screws from seizing and aid the setup of your bridge.

Keep a piece of clean cotton in your case and use this to wipe the strings down following each performance or practise, and use a string-care product such as Fast Fret to remove grease and grime from the strings while they are on the guitar. Do not forget to pass the cloth between the strings and the fingerboard. Rub graphite from a soft pencil into the slots in the nut of the guitar and under the string trees to aid the strings' movement in these areas. Use a fine needle file to remove burrs and other sharp edges from string posts and saddles.

Stretching Strings

Stretching new strings once they are on the guitar helps tuning stability. Tune the guitar to concert pitch and hold it on your knee in the playing position. Put the flat of your thumb under the low E string midway between the bridge and the nut while holding the neck of the guitar with your other hand. Firmly push the string away from the guitar two or three times. Repeat for each string. Do not worry about string breakage, if the string breaks during this process it was weak anyway and would not have lasted your next practise session. Re-tune and repeat until the strings hold tune after stretching.

Changing Broken Strings

BELOW: When changing a string on an acoustic guitar, first remove the pin which holds it in place.

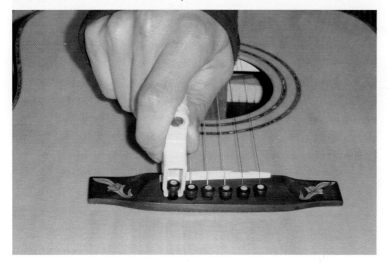

ABOVE: Once the new string has been inserted through the capstan, ensure enough slack has been left so that it can be would around the post.

BELOW: this is how the secure strings on an acoustic guitar should appear.

Acoustic Steel

Remove the broken string from the tuning machine. Ease a string-winding tool under the head of the bridge pin and use gentle downward pressure to lever the pin up and out of the bridge. Push the ball end of the fresh string into the empty hole and replace the pin. Note that the bridge pin has a groove in it to allow the string to pass by. The groove should face towards the soundhole.

Give the string a quick tug to ensure that the ball end is seated against the bottom of the pin, then pass the string through the capstan. There should be enough slack in the remaining string to allow it to be pulled about 7.5 cm (3 in) above the guitar. Use a string winder to wind neatly no more than four turns around the post. Plain strings may need more turns. Trim the excess string and tune.

Acoustic Nylon

Pass the new string through the bridge in the direction of the bottom of the guitar until 5 cm (2 in) of string is showing clear of the bridge. Bring the short end up and over the bridge and pass from left to right under the string on the other side. Weave through the string from left to right until three turns are trapped between the string and the bridge and tug the free string to make the end tight. Pass the string through the hole in the tuning gear and neatly wind as many turns as possible onto the post. Plain strings must be passed twice through the post to minimize slipping.

Electric, Stratocaster-Style Bridge

Dip the tremolo arm to align the string holes in the block with the rear cover. Shake the old ball end out or if necessary insert the end of the broken string through the bridge saddle and into the string hole from the front of the bridge to push it out. Take the fresh string and uncoil then push the plain end through the string hole in the bridge block at the rear of the guitar and up through the hole in the centre of the saddle.

Pull the remainder of the string through and tug firmly to ensure the ball end is seated in the bridge block. Pass the end of the string through the string post and take up the slack then pull back 2–3 cm (0.78–1.1 in) for turns. Gently pull the string away from the guitar as you wind the turns around the post. Tune and stretch.

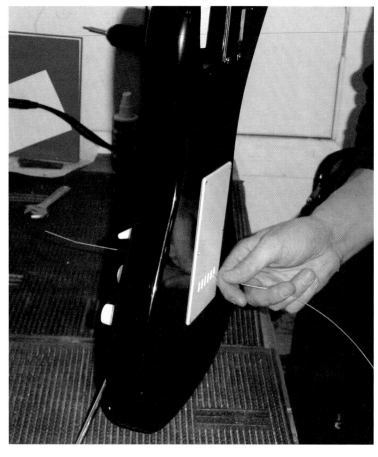

Gibson-Style Stop Tailpiece And Tune-O-Matic Bridge

ABOVE: Use a fast winder to wind the string around the post.

Pass the plain end of the string through the tailpiece and pull up to the headstock. Pass through the post then pull back 2–3 cm (0.78–1.1 in) for turns. Take the plain end and wrap clockwise around the post, pass under the string as it emerges from the post and pull up to trap the free end. Tune and stretch.

Setting The Action

String height (sometimes known as action) is important to the feel and therefore the playability of the guitar to the player. String height can be adjusted using adjustable bridge saddles on electric and some acoustic guitars. However, the optimum height of the string above the fingerboard is determined also by the depth of the nut slots and neck relief (the bow of the neck) therefore saddle height adjustment should always be followed by checking of neck relief and nut slot depth.

With the guitar on your knee, check neck relief by stopping the string at the first and twelfth fret and examining the gap between the bottom of the low E string and the top of the seventh fret. This should be about 0.013 in, enough to get a medium gauge plain string or a piece of thin card between them.

Play the guitar along the length of the neck and raise or lower height adjustable saddles to suit, periodically checking neck relief as you adjust each string. Check the depth of nut slots by stopping the string at the second fret and tapping the string between the nut and the first fret. You should hear a faint 'tick' as the string hits the top of the first fret. If you cannot hear anything it means that the slot is too deep. Extreme pressure means the slot is not deep enough.

Play along the neck again, adjust string height and check relief. Repeat until the guitar plays and feels satisfactory.

ABOVE: The action of a guitar significantly affects the sound: the higher the action, the louder the volume. Low action though is good for lead or fast riff work.

Adjusting The Nut

If the top nut becomes damaged it can be replaced with a new nut from your spares supplier. Beware, though, as many different nuts are available. Take your guitar to the store and try and get the best match. The new nut will require adjusting as the slots will require deepening to suit your guitar. Buy a set of diamond files and an Exacto saw from your local modelling supplier. Use the files for the wound string slots and the saw from the B and E strings slots. Make very small cuts until the required slot depth is achieved.

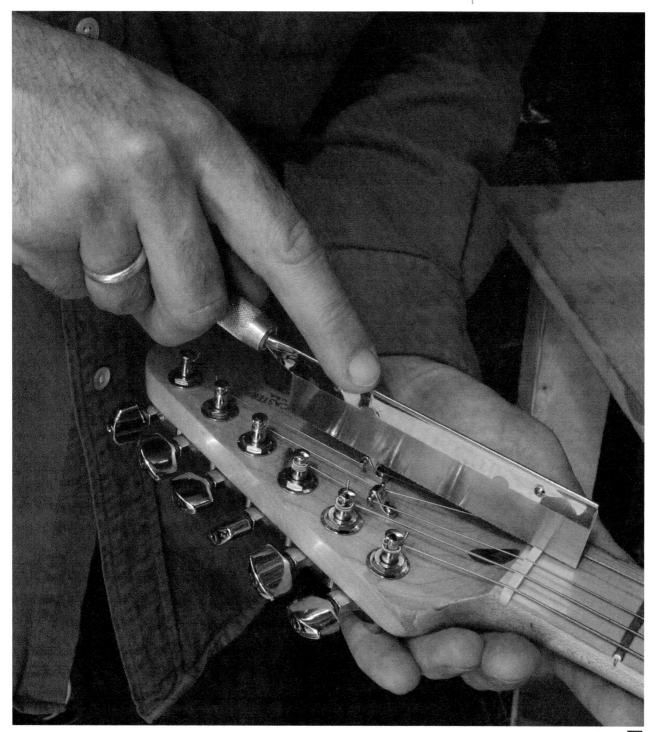

Setting Intonation

Intonation is the ability of the guitar to play in tune along the length of the neck. Because the strings of the guitar are different thicknesses, the length of each string has to be different to enable accurate intonation. Adjusting the intonation of the guitar is part of the guitar setup and should be carried out whenever changes are made to string gauge, neck relief or string height. Connect a good quality electronic guitar tuner to your guitar and lay flat on a clean surface. Play a harmonic note at the 12th fret (damp the string with the tip of your finger then remove it as you pluck the string) and note the reading at the tuner. Tighten or loosen the string using the tuning machines until the needle is dead centre. Play another harmonic note in the same place to recheck tuning. Stop the string at the 12th fret by pressing down on the string until it meets the fingerboard. Pluck the string and note the reading on the tuner: it should be dead centre. If not, move the saddle forward or backward using the adjustment screw. If the fretted note is flat, move the saddle forward. If sharp, move the saddle backwards. Check and repeat for each string.

Neck Adjustment

Truss rod or torque adjustment may be necessary if your guitar starts to buzz around the seventh fret or if string height appears to have changed in this area. The truss rod adjustment screw or nut is found under a plate at the base of the headstock or is clearly visible as a bullet on some Fender models. Some other Fender guitars require that the neck is removed to find the truss rod adjustment at the base of the neck. These are difficult to adjust as the strings and sometimes the scratchplate must be removed for access, and then replaced to check tension. Use a socket wrench or key of the correct fitting, and with the guitar tuned to concert pitch gently turn the nut less than one quarter turn in either direction (right to tighten or left to loosen).

The object is to create just enough space for the string to vibrate without buzzing. Tighten the rod for less space and loosen it for more space until the guitar is easy to play without string rattle. Check the tension of the neck by placing a straight edge along the frets between the 12th fret and the nut.

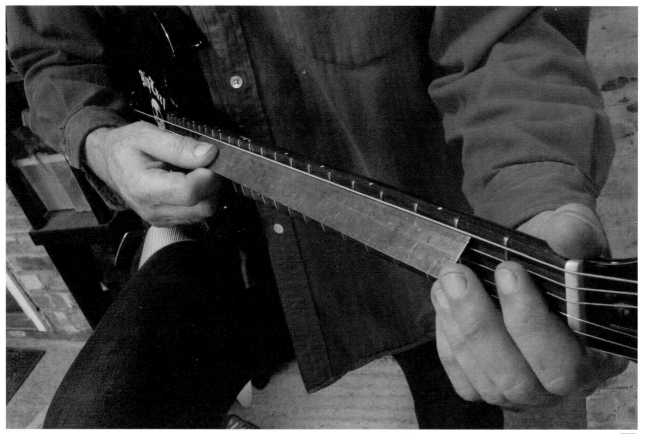

String Height Adjustments

Check and, if necessary, adjust intonation and string height each time a new set of strings is fitted. If moving from a different gauge, the intonation must be reset for each string. Correct string height is a matter of personal taste and dependent on the nature of your guitar.

Fender-style Bridge With Individual Saddles

Use the supplied hex wrench to raise or lower the height of each string saddle by turning the small height-adjustment screws in each saddle.

Gibson-Style ABS1 Tune-O-Matic Bridge With Adjustable Pillars

Raise or lower the height of the bridge by turning the milled thumb wheel under the bass or treble sides. Some models have a slotted screw head on the upper surface of the bridge, requiring a screwdriver to adjust it.

American-Standard Or Wilkinson-Style Bridge With Fulcrum And Pillars

Use the supplied hex key to raise or lower the bass and treble side of the bridge by screwing in or unscrewing each of the two retaining pillars at the front of the bridge.

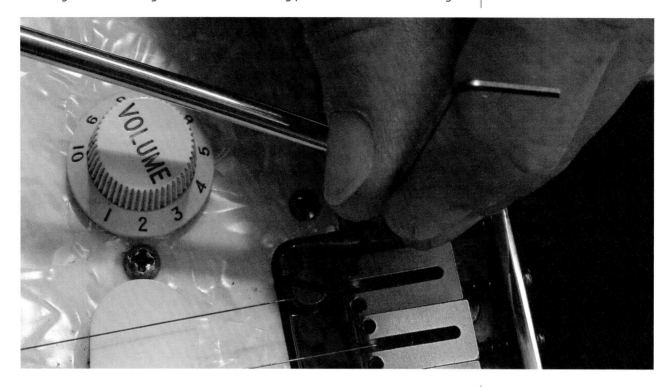

Intonation

Adjustments

BELOW: Intonation adjustment on a Fender Stratocaster.

These must be made after string height has been adjusted. Lay the guitar down and connect to a good-quality electronic guitar tuner. Play the open E string and adjust using the tuner until the string is in tune. Stop the string at the twelfth fret and note the pitch according to the tuner. This will indicate whether the intonation requires adjusting. If the tuner reads the same as the open string, then intonation for that string is perfect. If the tuner reads sharp or flat, the intonation will need adjusting.

For a flat string, using a screwdriver (or other tool) move the string saddle forward in the direction of the pickups. Adjust very slightly before checking the intonation, adjusting, rechecking etc., until both stopped and open strings read the same on the tuner. For a sharp string, follow the procedure as for a flat string but move the saddle backwards towards the bottom of the guitar.

Truss Rod Adjustment

ABOVE: Check for faults in the guitar's neck by looking along it.

Steel-strung acoustic and electric guitars have a steel truss rod fitted along the length of the neck underneath the fingerboard. This is held at tension to counteract the pull of the strings on the headstock. Its purpose is to maintain a slight bow in the neck to allow the string to vibrate at its widest point, while enabling the string height further up the neck to be as low as possible. The truss rod tension may need adjusting if the guitar has been left without maintenance for a number of years, or whenever a set of heavier or lighter strings are fitted.

Checking Truss Rod Tension

BELOW: Measure the guitar's action with a ruler. It should be no more than 0.013 in.

Hold the guitar in the playing position and using both hands fret the first and seventh fret. Look carefully at the small gap between the top of the seventh fret and the bottom of the low E string. This gap (or relief) should be no more than 0.035 cm (0.013 in) and can be measured using a set of spark gap feeler gauges, or a ruler. Alternatively, a fairly good rule of thumb is to use a standard-weight business card. If the card can be slipped between the seventh fret and the string then the truss rod tension is satisfactory. Bass guitars require more relief. To adjust the truss rod it is necessary to find the adjustable nut at the end of the rod. On some Fender guitars this is a clearly visible 'bullet' behind the nut.

Gibson and other guitars have a plate on the headstock, which must be removed. Some Telecasters and other similar guitars require that the neck be removed to gain access to the slotted key at the end of the neck. This job is best left to a professional.

If the neck has too much relief, the truss rod must be tightened by using the supplied key or wrench to turn the nut clockwise. Less than a quarter turn is required. As always, adjust and recheck until the correct adjustments have been made. A neck with too little relief requires that the truss rod be loosened slightly by turning the nut anticlockwise. Again, use a very small adjustment and constantly recheck.

In general, always adjust the rod with the guitar tuned to concert pitch and in the playing position. Never force the adjustment. If the truss rod nut will not turn, the guitar should be taken to a professional. Too much tension can snap the rod and then the fingerboard will need removing to replace it.

ABOVE: Fender Stratocaster-style truss rod.

LEFT: Gibson Les Paul-style truss rod.

Guitar Electronics

ABOVE: Inside view of a humbucker pickup.

Circuits and components used in mass-produced production guitars largely remain unchanged from their origins in post-war America, where the principles of guitar electronics – simple wire coils and magnets – were widely understood and employed in telephone and loudspeaker manufacture. A disturbance in the magnetic field of a magnet will cause a current to flow through a coil of wire wrapped tightly around the magnet. The direction of the current will change depending on the direction of the force exerted on the magnet. A vibrating string moves towards and then away from the magnet, causing the flow to travel in one direction and then the other. This produces alternating current. The current from the pickup can be passed through other components, such as volume and tone controls, before it is amplified.

A guitar pickup is an assembly of magnets, wire and magnetic pole pieces designed to capture and convert the vibration of the guitar strings into current as efficiently as possible. Pickups placed closer to the bridge of the guitar will create a brighter sound than pickups placed closer to the centre of the guitar. If more than one pickup is fixed to the guitar, switches may be used to select and change the electric sound of the guitar.

BELOW: The basic electronic components of the electric guitar: switches and pickups.

Tools And Equipment For Electrical Repairs

It is possible to equip yourself to handle the majority of electrical tasks on your guitar with just a few inexpensive tools. A good-quality No. 2 Philips screwdriver and a small electrical flat blade screwdriver are essential. A pair of wire cutters can be used for cutting wires and for cutting and trimming strings. A pair of needle pliers is useful for handling components and for holding parts steady when soldering.

All parts inside the guitar have soldered connections which can and do break. Buy a good-quality, medium wattage iron and electrical solder. Practise your soldering on a few offcuts first before going to work on your instrument. No dangerous voltages exist inside the electric guitar, but always use safety goggles when soldering and remember to keep the hot iron in a safe place while working. A small adjustable wrench is very useful for removing controls and tightening loose sockets.

Finally, buy a can of Servisol for cleaning inside pots (control knobs) and for good jack socket connections. Always sketch the layout of controls and switches, noting where each connection is made, colour-coding them if necessary before you start. It is much easier to recover from a mistake if you have a simple map.

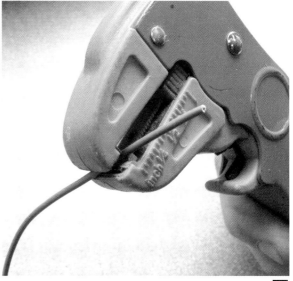

Wiring

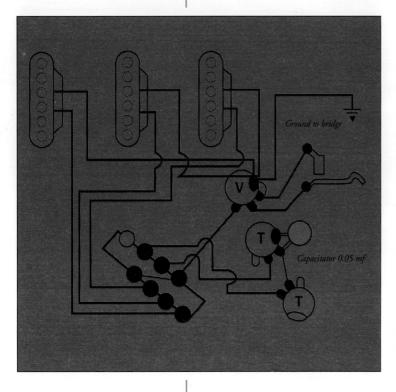

Ground to bridge

Capacitator 0.05 mf

Stratocaster

The single coil pickups fitted to every Stratocaster use a very simple two-conductor cable. On American and vintage models these are coded white for 'hot' and black for 'ground'. The five-way selector switch requires a jumper to enable the switching options, quality single conductor cable is used, as the short length means that the cable is easily damaged when applying heat. Two-conductor screened cable is used for the connection between the jack socket and the rear of the volume control. This is the only place that screened cable is used in the Stratocaster. Volume and tone pots are 250 K, the capacitor is a 0.05 mf ceramic.

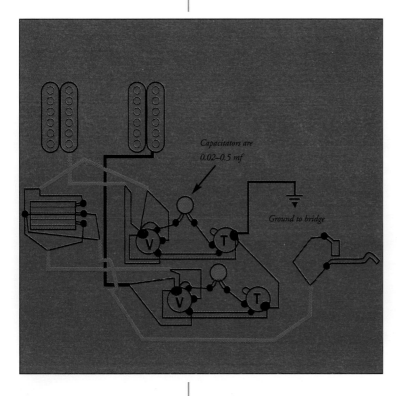

Capacitators are 0.02–0.5 mf

Ground to bridge

Les Paul Standard

The Les Paul Standard is fitted with Gibson 490T and 490R pickups. These are two conductor pickups but unlike the Stratocaster the ground conductor is braided around the hot conductor forming a screen. A length of screened cable is also used to connect the jack socket to the switch. The specification for screened cable and humbucking pickups means that the Les Paul suffers much less from RF (radio frequency) interference and is one reason why it is a popular recording guitar. Volume and tone pots are 500 K and the tone capacitor are 0.2 mf ceramic.

Replacing A Stratocaster- Style Pickup

Pickup replacement of a simple two-conductor pickup is a simple job that brings enormous benefits to the sound and value of your instrument. Replacement pickups of a much better quality than those fitted to most budget Far Eastern guitars can be purchased for around £30.

To replace a pickup, first remove the strings and scratchplate screws. Store in a small bag for safe keeping. Trace the two conductors from the rear of the pickup to be replaced to the components on the underside of the scratchplate.

Cut each wire carefully, leaving a small amount still attached to the guitar. This makes it much easier to identify the correct tags later on. Remove the height-adjustment screws and catch the two springs that will now be free. Remove the pickup from the hole. Assemble the new pickup and scratchplate using either the screws supplied or the original parts. Take the two conductors and trim 5 mm (0.2 in) of insulation from each. Carefully tin the bare ends with hot solder. Unsolder the remaining hot conductor from the underside of the pickup selector switch and make the tag ready for the new conductor. Solder the hot (white, or centre) conductor to the tag. Free the remaining ground wire from the rear of the volume control and replace with the new (black, or screen) ground wire. Attach the scratchplate to the guitar and refit the strings.

Note that some manufacturers use different colour coding, so check the instructions before fitting. Before replacing the scratchplate, test the new pickup by connecting the guitar to an amp and lightly tapping the polepices of the new pickup with a key or similar.

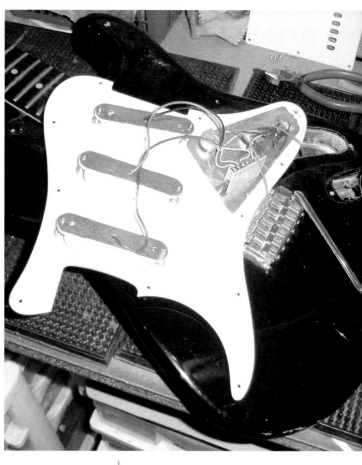

BELOW: Before replacing the new pickup, it will need to be assembled.

45

Replacing A Humbucker Pickup

Remove the strings from the guitar and expose all cavities. Make a simple sketch of all parts and connections before carefully snipping the existing connections leading from the pickup you are replacing to the rear of the volume pot or switch depending on model. Unsolder ground wire. Remove the four screws from the pickup mounting ring and set aside. Gently pull the pickup from the guitar, note the orientation of cables to the mounting ring and guitar before removing height adjustment screws and springs then set aside. Offer the new pickup to the mounting ring and attach using height adjustment screws and springs. Feed the pickup wire through the body and pull from the rear until the pickup is seated correctly in the body. Note that the pickup is mounted and orientated correctly before reattaching pickup assembly to the guitar using four mounting ring screws. Refer to the manufacturers instructions then unsolder remaining old pickup wire from guitar before replacing with hot wire from new pickup. Solder ground connection to rear of volume pot. Attach strings, check function then replace control plates. Adjust the height of new pickup using height adjustment screws allowing for stronger magnetic pull from the new pickup.

Replacing A Jack Socket On A Fender-Style Guitar

The jack sockets are the parts of your guitar most vulnerable to damage. Replacing a broken or worn socket is a simple job that can save a great deal of trouble.

Remove the two screws holding the recessed jack plate to the guitar then remove the old socket by releasing the nut holding the socket to the plate.

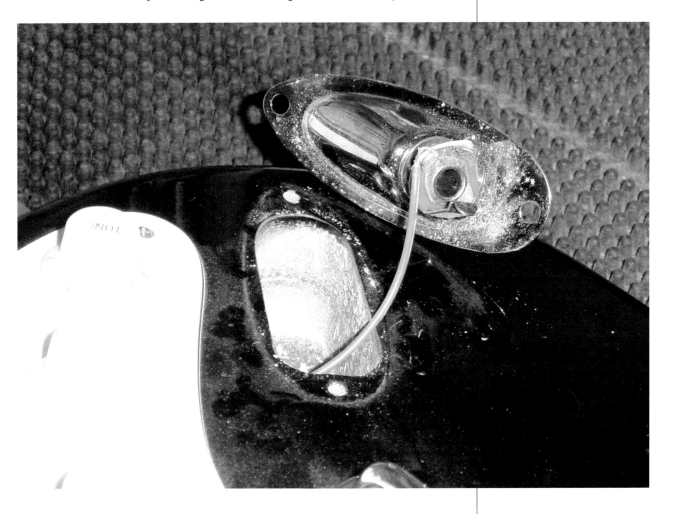

Cut away the ground and hot conductors as close as possible to the solder joints.

Trim and strip away 10 mm (0.3 in) of insulation from the cable, then strip 3 mm (0.1 in) of insulation from the centre conductor. Solder the screen of the cable to the tag connected to the ring of the socket. Solder the hot (centre) connector to the tag connected to the tip of the socket.

Replace the jack socket in the socket plate and attach to the top of the guitar.

Index